THE CURRENTS OF CHANGE

How to Thrive During Corporate Transitions

SHARON GROSSMAN, PHD

WARRIOR
PUBLISHING

Warrior Publishing, LLC
drsharongrossman.com/contact
ISBN 978-1-952437-03-8

Contents

Chapter 1: Disrupted Routine and Salty Surprises .. 1

Chapter 2: Unexpected Catch 5

Chapter 3: Merger Mayhem 10

Chapter 4: When Worlds Collide 14

Chapter 5: The Rhino Roars (and Other Concerns
 Addressed) 18

Chapter 6: Unlikely Connections........................... 23

Chapter 7 : Collaborative Catastrophes.................. 27

Chapter 8: Building the Blueprint.......................... 31

Chapter 9: Synergy in Action................................. 35

Chapter 10: Celebrating Milestones....................... 39

Chapter 11: Embracing New Horizons.................. 45

Epilogue: The Roadmap for Navigating Change... 50

About the Author... 60

CHAPTER 1

Disrupted Routine and Salty Surprises

The familiar buzz of her alarm clock was almost comforting on a Saturday morning. Clara Calamity stretched luxuriously, the early sunlight painting a warm stripe across her tiny apartment. Saturday mornings were for indulging in the simple pleasures – a leisurely breakfast, a good book, and most importantly, a refreshing swim at the local pool.

Slipping into her bright pink swimsuit, a beacon of cheer in the still-sleepy apartment, Clara hummed along to the chirping birds outside. Today, after her swim, she planned to finally tackle the mountain of unpacked boxes that still dominated her living space. With a spring in her step, she grabbed her towel and headed out the door.

The brisk morning air invigorated her as she walked towards the pool. Reaching the familiar blue fence, a frown creased her forehead. A large banner plastered across the gate announced the pool's closure for "exciting renovations." "Cascading waterfalls" and "subterranean grottos" promised a "reimagined aquatic experience." Clara snorted. "Subterranean grottos? More like upgraded annoyance," she muttered. Disappointment settled in her stomach. The pool was her sanctuary, a place where she could clear her head and unwind after a long week.

Dejected, she turned back towards her apartment, the mental image of her empty pool lane replaced by a looming pile of boxes. As she unlocked the door, a booming voice startled her. "Clara Calamity!" boomed Mr. Bluster, the building manager, his handlebar mustache bristling like an irate caterpillar. "About that leaky faucet you mentioned..."

Clara winced, remembering the sheepish email she'd sent the night before after the persistent drip had kept her up most of the night. A placating smile spread across her face. "Good morning, Mr. Bluster! Come in, come in."

Mr. Bluster shuffled in, disapproval radiating off him like heat waves. "Should've called a plumber, you know. These things can be tricky." He eyed her swimsuit with suspicion. "You sure you're not heading out again already?"

Clara sighed. "Unfortunately not, Mr. Bluster. The pool's closed for renovations."

Mr. Bluster grunted noncommittally and followed her towards the bathroom, muttering something about "young people these days" and the "dangers of DIY disasters." As Clara explained the faucet situation, she couldn't help but think about the disrupted routine, the unpacked boxes, and the general feeling of being thrown off track.

Just as Mr. Bluster tightened the last screw with a grunt of satisfaction, her phone buzzed. It was a message from Michelle, her best friend. "Hey! Beach day? Sun's out, waves are rolling, and the ice cream shop by the pier is calling my name!"

Clara stared at the message. A beach day wasn't exactly what she'd planned, but then again, neither was a leaky faucet or a closed pool. Looking down, she realized she was still in her swimsuit. Maybe, just maybe, this disrupted Saturday wouldn't be a complete write-off after all.

"Hey, thanks, sounds great!" she typed back, a smile returning to her face. "Meet you there in half an hour?"

With a quick goodbye to Mr. Bluster and a promise to call a real plumber for future emergencies, Clara grabbed her beach bag and headed out the door. The ocean, vast and untamed, stretched before her, a stark contrast to the predictable lanes of the pool. A sense of adventure bubbled up in her stomach, replacing the earlier disappointment. Maybe this "reimagined aquatic experience" wouldn't be so bad after all. She might even find a new way to love the water.

CHAPTER 2

Unexpected Catch

The salty breeze whipped through Clara's hair as she navigated the bustling boardwalk, her bright pink swimsuit a pop of color amongst the white beach umbrellas. Spotting Michelle perched on a lifeguard stand, a towel wrapped around her shoulders, a smile bloomed on Clara's face. This unexpected beach trip might be just what she needed to clear her head after the morning's disappointments.

As she approached, Michelle waved enthusiastically. "Clara! There you are! I snagged us the perfect spot – front row seats to the ocean's greatest show!"

Clara plopped down beside her, kicking off her flip-flops and burying her toes in the warm sand. "Thanks for the invite," she said, letting out a sigh of relief. "Honestly, I could really use a break from unpacking boxes and… well, the whole merger mess at work."

She trailed off, realizing she'd almost blurted out her anxieties about the upcoming merger with BioRhythmic Devices. The new company culture, the potential changes to her workload, the sheer unknown of it all – it was a constant knot of tension in her stomach.

But before she could delve into her worries, Michelle cut her off. "Merger schmerger! Today is all about the beach! Sun, sand, and of course..." she pointed towards the crashing waves, "a swim in the glorious ocean!"

Clara felt a pang of disappointment. Venting about work had seemed like a good idea, but clearly, Michelle had other plans. "Actually," Clara began hesitantly, "I'm not really an ocean swimmer. I prefer the predictability of lanes and the controlled environment of a pool."

Michelle's eyes widened. "A pool person? On a beach day? Come on, Calamity! Live a little!" she teased, nudging Clara playfully.

Clara laughed, but her hesitation remained. "Look, I can't exactly do the butterfly stroke in the ocean," she admitted. "And what about all the... stuff? Seaweed, jellyfish..."

Michelle rolled her eyes. "Relax, drama queen. Just a quick dip, that's all. See that rocky point over there?" she pointed towards a distant landmark jutting out into the ocean. "Swim there and back. I'll be waiting for you, sun goddess style."

Clara stared at the distant point, then back at Michelle's expectant gaze. A small, adventurous part of her felt a tug of excitement. Maybe a little ocean adventure wouldn't hurt. Taking a deep breath, she nodded.

"Alright, alright," she conceded, a hint of determination in her voice. "Just don't expect any Olympic-worthy speed here."

With that, she stood up, peeled off her cover-up, and waded into the cool water. The waves, playful at first, grew stronger as she ventured further out and began swimming toward the point. She sputtered and laughed, the rhythmic rise and fall of the ocean a welcome change from the monotony of her apartment walls.

Suddenly, a sharp tug on her wrist sent a jolt through her. Realizing she was caught on something, she stopped swimming. Looking down, she saw a thin fishing line wrapped tightly around her wrist. Following the line, she saw a young man on the beach, his attention fixed on a cooler at his feet.

"Hey!" Clara called out, her voice battling the waves. "Think you might have the wrong catch!" she added, a touch of humor lacing her voice despite the situation.

The young man whipped his head up, startled. A flush of embarrassment painted his cheeks as he realized his mistake. "Oh my gosh, I'm so sorry!" he yelled back, scrambling to reel in the line and free Clara's wrist. "Are you alright?"

Clara flashed a reassuring smile, shaking her head. "Just a bit tangled in your line, that's all."

The young man, still flustered, muttered apologies before quickly adding, "Enjoy your swim!"

With a wave of her hand, Clara resumed her journey. Reaching the rocky point, she collapsed onto the warm sand, heart pounding. Michelle soon joined her, a wide grin on her face.

"See? Told you it wouldn't be boring!" she exclaimed. Clara recounted her harrowing encounter with the fishing line, relief tinged with amusement.

As they sat there, laughing, Clara realized this beach trip had been exactly what she needed, even if not in the way she'd originally planned. It wasn't a chance to vent about work, but it was a much-needed escape, a chance to face a small fear and laugh about it afterwards. Maybe, just maybe, the upcoming merger wouldn't be so bad either. After all, a little unexpected adventure could be just the thing to shake things up.

CHAPTER 3

Merger Mayhem

Monday morning arrived with the efficiency of a well-oiled machine, a stark contrast to the chaotic state of Clara's emotions. Excitement for the "synergistic" merger had been replaced by a gnawing anxiety. Walking through the office doors, she was greeted by a cacophony of unfamiliar voices and the pungent aroma of what smelled suspiciously like patchouli oil.

Gone were the neat rows of cubicles and beige walls. The BioRhythmic team had apparently transformed their allotted space into a haven of mismatched furniture, beanbag chairs, and a whiteboard adorned with multicolored scribbles that resembled a modern art exhibit gone wrong. A woman with a mane of purple hair and a nose ring greeted her with a booming laugh. "Hey there, you must be Clara! I'm Luna, resident data whisperer and BioRhythmic's secret weapon!"

Clara, ever the optimist, offered a hesitant smile. "Nice to meet you, Luna." Across the room, a stern-faced woman in a power suit tapped her foot impatiently. This must be Ms. Thornberry, the BioRhythmic CEO, whose reputation for ruthless efficiency preceded her.

The morning meeting was a clash of cultures – spreadsheets versus vision boards, conservative suits versus tie-dye shirts. Ms. Thornberry droned on about "disruptive innovation" while Clara's boss, Mr. Peabody, meticulously outlined data migration protocols. Eyes glazed over, tempers flared, and by the end of the meeting, Clara felt like she'd been caught in a verbal tennis match with no clear winner.

As the BioRhythmic team retreated to their aromatic haven, Mr. Peabody emerged from his office, a grimace etched on his face. "Welcome to the new normal, Calamity," he sighed. "We'll need all hands on deck to navigate this cultural clash."

Just then, a tall man with an easy smile and a name tag that read "Dr. Evans" entered the room. "Mr. Peabody? Clara?" he said, his voice radiating a calming energy. "I'm Dr. Evans, the change management consultant assigned to help you navigate this merger."

A collective sigh of relief rippled through the room. Dr. Evans launched into a clear and concise explanation of the merger plan. "We have a shared vision," he explained, "to create a streamlined, data-driven organization that fosters innovation. Our goals are to bridge the cultural gap, develop clear communication channels, and provide targeted training to address any skill gaps."

He continued: "We'll be implementing a series of workshops to foster communication and build trust between the teams. Regular progress updates and open forums will ensure everyone feels involved in the process." Relief washed over Clara. This wasn't just empty promises of "synergy"; Dr. Evans had a plan, a clear vision, and a structured approach to navigate the merger madness.

"Of course," Dr. Evans concluded with a twinkle in his eye, "there will be challenges. But together, we can transform this merger from a clash of cultures into a fusion of forces."

Clara glanced across the room at Luna, whose head was now buried in a book titled "The Power of Positive Collaboration." Maybe, just maybe, Dr. Evans' optimistic vision wouldn't be so far-fetched after all. The merger might still hold uncertainties, but with a roadmap and a change management expert steering the ship, Clara felt a flicker of hope. The unexpected ocean adventure had taught her to embrace a little chaos. Maybe this merger, with all its quirks and conflicts, could be the unexpected adventure her career needed.

CHAPTER 4

When Worlds Collide

A hush fell over the conference room as Dr. Evans, his smile as bright as a button, clapped his hands together. Gone were the stuffy suits and the whiteboard scribbles. In their place, a vibrant menagerie of inflatable animals now adorned the walls – a zebra, a giraffe, and a particularly grumpy-looking rhino that seemed to glare at Ms. Thornberry.

"Welcome back, everyone!" Dr. Evans boomed, his voice filled with an infectious enthusiasm. "Today, we embark on a wondrous journey – the grand merging of BioRhythmic Devices and HealthNex Solutions! But before we set sail on this uncharted sea of innovation," he paused for dramatic effect, "let's address the elephant in the room, or perhaps," he gestured towards the inflatable rhino, "the grumpy rhino in the corner."

A ripple of confused laughter went through the room. Ms. Thornberry, however, remained unfazed, her expression a stoic mask. Dr. Evans continued, launching into an unexpected analogy.

"Imagine," he said, his voice dropping to a conspiratorial whisper, "we are both fantastical creatures. BioRhythmic, the nimble gazelle, swift and innovative. HealthNex Solutions, a majestic elephant, wise and grounded in data. Alone, we are formidable. But together?" He spread his arms wide, knocking over a stack of paperwork in the process. A few papers fluttered to the floor, landing at Ms. Thornberry's feet like errant autumn leaves.

Ms. Thornberry, ever the picture of composure, simply bent down and retrieved them without a word. Dr. Evans, oblivious, continued. "Together, we are a magnificent griffin, a mythical beast combining the strength of a lion and the grace of an eagle!" He pointed to a hastily drawn picture of a griffin on the whiteboard, complete with rainbow wings and a sparkly crown. Clara couldn't help but stifle a giggle.

"Why merge, you ask?" Dr. Evans continued, his voice returning to its normal volume. "Because, dear friends, this griffin will soar! We will create groundbreaking medical technology, revolutionize patient care, and leave a legacy that will make history sing our praises!"

He then launched into the details of the merger, his explanations peppered with imaginative metaphors and colorful charts resembling children's pop-up books. Timelines unfolded like intricate castles, leadership structures resembled a playful family tree with titles like "Chief Innovation Cheetah" and "Director of Data Doves," and potential departmental changes were laid out as a game board for employees to navigate.

Throughout the presentation, Dr. Evans encouraged questions, his responses delivered with a charming charm that even managed to crack a smile on Ms. Thornberry's face (although it was a very small smile, barely perceptible to the naked eye). He detailed various training plans, communication channels modeled after a crystal-clear mountain stream, and feedback mechanisms designed to be as clear as a babbling brook.

By the end of the presentation, the room buzzed with a different kind of energy. Confusion and apprehension were replaced by a cautious curiosity. The griffin analogy, though undeniably odd, had somehow managed to convey the potential of the merger. The unexpected, quirky way Dr. Evans had presented the plan had sparked a flicker of hope.

Could this fantastical creature, this griffin of innovation, take flight after all?

CHAPTER 5

The Rhino Roars (and Other Concerns Addressed)

The initial charm of Dr. Evans' Wondrous Merger Menagerie had faded like a novelty sticker losing its stick. Tuesday morning brought a brutal reality check. Clara sat in a training session, surrounded by a sea of unfamiliar faces, the once-uplifting chirping metaphor for communication now grating on her nerves.

The new data management system loomed over them like a complex, labyrinthine beast. Confusion morphed into frustration as the training progressed. The user interface, designed by a team of overzealous colorblind monkeys according to one disgruntled murmur, seemed more likely to induce migraines than productivity.

Suddenly, a voice erupted, shattering the tense silence. Ms. Thornberry slammed her hand on the table. "This is utter chaos!" she boomed, her voice a rallying cry in the storm of discontent. "This system is a bureaucratic nightmare! It will devour our time and leave our patients waiting!"

Her outburst, while shocking, unleashed a torrent of pent-up anxieties. A chorus of concerns echoed through the room – data security vulnerabilities, plummeting productivity during the transition, and the most dreaded specter of all – job redundancy.

Dr. Evans glanced at the inflatable rhino, its thick hide and determined expression mirroring the room's collective unease. "Your concerns are valid, and we appreciate you voicing them. And, I assure you that we will address them all…but before we do, let's all take a collective breath."

The room seemed to settle just a bit, the breath grounding their anxiety.

"If I may play psychologist for just a moment," said Dr. Evans, "the uncertainty and lack of familiarity of these changes has gotten us all wound up. To your point, Ms. Thornberry, the last thing we want is to increase our workload unnecessarily or to keep our patients waiting. We certainly want both our company data and our jobs to be secure. These are important without a doubt. But sometimes, if we focus too much on the "what ifs," we can become unhinged.

You know, the Rhino have been around for millions of years. Their ancestors roamed the Earth alongside dinosaurs. We don't exactly know how this happened, but, just a guess, it may have been their thick skin. It's up to 1.5 inches thick in some areas, helping them regulate their body temperature. I see you all like a group of rhinos, resilient and tenacious.

He then launched into a detailed response, addressing each concern head-on. He outlined a phased rollout of the new system, with extensive training and support offered at every step. Data security, he assured them, was a top priority, with robust measures in place.

However, the looming threat of job redundancy cast a shadow over the room. John, a young man from BioRhythmic spoke up, his voice trembling slightly. "What about overlap in our roles? Will some of us be... let go?"

Dr. Evans' smile faltered for a moment. He admitted that some streamlining might occur, but he emphasized that the focus would be on reskilling and upskilling employees to fit the needs of the new organization. He reassured them of a transparent process with ample severance packages for any unforeseen departures.

Clara, however, found little comfort in these reassurances. While the others seemed mollified, a nagging worry gnawed at her. Her role involved a specific data analysis technique that BioRhythmic didn't seem to utilize. Would her skillset become obsolete? Would she be the odd one out, the expendable cog in the grand merger machine?

Despite Dr. Evans' words, her biggest fear remained a silent, festering wound. As the training session ended, the camaraderie Clara had felt earlier seemed to dissipate. The path ahead remained shrouded in uncertainty, a tangled web of data migration, cultural clashes, and new systems to navigate. The griffin, once a symbol of shared potential, now felt like a precarious creature, its wings flapping uncertainly against the winds of change.

Clara left the training room, the weight of her unspoken concern heavy in her heart. She wasn't sure what the future held, but one thing was clear – the merger might be a wondrous adventure for Dr. Evans, but for her, it felt more like a tightrope walk over a bed of hungry crocodiles.

CHAPTER 6

Unlikely Connections

The elevator groaned to a sluggish halt at Clara Calamity's floor. Stepping inside, she was greeted by a new face – a tall, weathered man. His face held a map of wrinkles, etched by years of experience.

Clara, eager for some peace before tackling the ocean waves and the even-more-daunting merger waves, offered a friendly smile. "Good morning," she chirped.

The man glanced up, a hint of amusement crinkling the corners of his eyes. "Haven't seen you around these parts before," he rumbled, his voice surprisingly gentle for such a burly fellow.

"Just moved in," Clara explained, gesturing towards her new apartment with her thumb. "My name's Clara."

He extended a hand, his grip firm but not crushing. "Seamus, at your service. Welcome to the building, Clara. Top floor, quietest place in the whole joint, except for the occasional rogue pigeon on the balcony."

Clara chuckled, shaking his hand. "Sounds perfect. I couldn't help but notice that pattern on your shirt. It's a Fibonacci sequence, isn't it?"

Seamus' eyebrows shot up in surprise. "You noticed that? Most people just see a bunch of squiggles."

Clara smiled. "I can't help it, I'm a data analyst. Patterns are kind of my thing."

The man chuckled, a sound like pebbles tumbling down a drainpipe. "Aye, missy. Used to be a data analyst myself, back in the day. Before these fancy computers stole all the fun."

Clara's eyes widened. "Really? A data analyst?" The unexpected revelation sparked a flicker of interest in her.

"Aye," he winked, a twinkle in his eye. "Numbers, they're like stubborn mules. They might buck and bray, but eventually, they'll walk the path you lead them down."

The elevator doors pinged open, interrupting their conversation.

"Nice meeting you, Seamus," she said, stepping out. "See you around."

He gave her a nod. "Good luck with the new place, Clara. And with whatever life throws your way."

Clara smiled, feeling a strange sense of connection with this gruff but insightful stranger. Maybe this new building, and this new city, wouldn't be so bad after all.

Reaching the beach, she stripped down to her swimsuit, the cool water embracing her like a comforting hug. As she pushed off from the shore, her mind drifted back to the man in the elevator. His words, seasoned with experience, echoed in her head.

Change, a tricky beast he'd called it. And he was right. The merger felt like a monstrous wave threatening to knock her off balance. Would her skills translate to the new company? Would she even have a job? The questions raced through her mind.

Taking a deep breath, she remembered the man's metaphor. She was the one in control of the numbers, not the other way around. Even the mightiest oak, she reminded herself, started as a tiny acorn, weathering storms and adapting to its environment. Just like the ocean, vast and ever-changing, she too could adapt. If it wasn't at the present company, she'd find her way elsewhere.

With renewed determination, she dove beneath the surface, the cool water washing away some of her anxieties. The rhythmic crash of the waves became a mantra – change, adapt, overcome. The vastness of the ocean mirrored the possibilities, not the problems, that lay before her. Maybe this merger wouldn't drown her after all, but carry her to a new and exciting shore.

CHAPTER 7

Collaborative Catastrophes

On Wednesday morning, Clara arrived at the office for the much-anticipated "Craft Trainings Related to the Plan" session with a cautious optimism. Dr. Evans' enthusiastic emails promised an engaging team-building exercise to foster collaboration. However, the aroma wafting from the conference room wasn't exactly conducive to a productive meeting. It smelled suspiciously like overripe bananas and something vaguely resembling burnt toast.

As she entered the room, a scene of controlled chaos unfolded before her. Ms. Thornberry stood beside a table overflowing with a motley crew of ingredients: flour, eggs, an alarmingly green tub of what might have been guacamole, and a precariously balanced stack of pre-made pizza dough. Across the room, Luna sported a headband adorned with a single, wilted carrot and was vigorously stirring a vat of what looked suspiciously like neon-orange mashed potatoes.

"Welcome, everyone!" Dr. Evans boomed, his voice surprisingly cheerful given the impending disaster. "Today, we embark on a collaborative culinary quest! Each team will create a dish that embodies the essence of our unified vision!"

A collective groan rippled through the room. It turned out, Dr. Evans' "Craft Trainings" involved a bizarre team-building exercise where departments were to create "synergy snacks" using a random selection of ingredients.

Confusion reigned supreme. A heated debate erupted about whether to utilize the questionable guacamole in a "data-driven dip" or a "patient-pleasing pesto." Ms. Thornberry, with a stoicism that bordered on heroic, glared at a jar of pickled eggs like a seasoned general sizing up a particularly obstinate enemy battalion.

Clara found herself paired with Mr. Peabody, her boss, and a young BioRhythmic engineer named Raj, whose enthusiasm for the challenge was inversely proportional to his understanding of the difference between baking powder and baking soda.

As the minutes ticked by, the room descended into organized chaos. Flour fights erupted over the hunt for mixing bowls. Luna, attempting to create "nutritious nanobites" with a food processor that resembled a disgruntled robot, ended up spraying the room with a fine mist of green mashed potato. Clara's attempt at a "data-driven dough" resulted in a lumpy, misshapen blob that defied categorization.

Just when it seemed like the situation couldn't get any worse, the fire alarm blared, triggered by a rogue spark from a malfunctioning toaster oven. The room erupted in a panicked frenzy, a comical mix of flour-dusted faces and singed eyebrows making a hasty retreat.

Later, huddled on the sidewalk outside the building, the tension eased into a wave of hysterical laughter. The exercise, despite its disastrous outcome, had achieved something unexpected – a sense of camaraderie amidst the merger madness. Ms. Thornberry, even she, was seen sporting a faint smile as she shook a fistful of flour from her immaculate blazer.

Back in the conference room, after the fire department deemed the culprit a faulty toaster, Dr. Evans declared the exercise a success. "Though the snacks may not have been award-winning," he said with a chuckle, "we've learned a valuable lesson:

communication, collaboration, and maybe a good fire extinguisher are key ingredients to a successful merger!"

As Clara left for the day, the disastrous team-building exercise still fresh in her mind, she realized something. The merger might be a chaotic recipe with unpredictable ingredients, but with a dash of humor, a sprinkle of teamwork, and maybe a healthy dose of fire drills, they might just create something edible after all.

CHAPTER 8

Building the Blueprint

The echo of Dr. Evans' enthusiastic pronouncements about fostering a unified company culture still lingered in the air. However, the task of translating that vision into tangible action fell on the shoulders of the team leaders – a diverse group from both BioRhythmic and HealthNex Solutions. They gathered around a conference table, faces etched with lingering anxieties about the merger.

Dr. Evans, ever the facilitator, kicked things off with a simple question: "What are the core values we want to see reflected in our daily work?"

A thoughtful silence descended upon the room. Ms. Thornberry, BioRhythmic's CEO, spoke first, her voice firm. "Efficiency is paramount. We need streamlined processes that minimize waste and maximize results." Heads nodded in agreement.

Rajiv, a young and energetic engineer from HealthNex, chimed in, "Innovation shouldn't be stifled! We need to encourage new ideas, even the seemingly crazy ones." A chuckle rippled through the room, a flicker of camaraderie emerging.

Clara added, "Data is the lifeblood of our decisions. We need to embrace data-driven insights and share them openly."

The ideas flowed freely – collaboration, respect for diverse perspectives, exceeding expectations, and fostering a supportive environment. Each leader contributed a piece of the puzzle, their shared experiences weaving a tapestry of what they hoped the new company culture would be.

As the conversation progressed, Dr. Evans, with that twinkle in his eye, began scribbling on a whiteboard. He captured the essence of their discussion in a series of concise phrases:

- **S**treamlined Processes: I eliminate redundancies.
- **Y**our Data Matters: I use data to make decisions and share insights.
- **N**urture Innovation: I welcome new ideas and calculated risks.
- **E**veryone Works Together: I communicate and collaborate with my colleagues. **R**espectful Interactions: I treat everyone with dignity and welcome diversity.
- **G**o the Extra Mile: I exceed expectations.
- **Y**our Feedback is Valuable: I share timely feedback and constructive criticism with my team.

He looked up, a triumphant grin on his face. "Behold! The S.Y.N.E.R.G.Y. principles! These are the building blocks of our new culture, a foundation for collaboration and success."

The team leaders studied the acronym, a sense of ownership settling over them. These weren't just Dr. Evans' crazy ideas; these were the values they had collectively defined. They would not just be words on a board; they would be a guiding light, a way to evaluate performance, and a framework for building a truly unified company.

Leaving the meeting room, a newfound sense of purpose propelled them forward. The road ahead was still uncertain, but they were no longer a group of strangers navigating a merger. They were now a team, united by a shared vision and the S.Y.N.E.R.G.Y. principles that would guide them towards a successful future.

CHAPTER 9

Synergy in Action

The S.Y.N.E.R.G.Y. principles gleamed on the conference room whiteboard, a mantra for the new company culture Clara was determined to cultivate. Bridging the gap between BioRhythmic's established processes and HealthNex Solutions' innovative spirit felt like navigating a white-water rapids course. Their first joint project – a pilot program to assess the effectiveness of a new sleep tracker in managing chronic fatigue – was a microcosm of the larger challenge.

From Clara's perspective, the room crackled with tension. Dr. Evans meticulously reviewed protocols with Luna. A stickler for detail, Luna mirrored Dr. Evans' furrowed brow with each line item. Across the table, Rajeev bounced in his seat, his backpack overflowing with prototype trackers. His unbridled enthusiasm, while infectious, threatened to derail the conversation with each new, albeit creative, suggestion.

Sarah, with her dry wit, leaned over to Clara and whispered, "This feels less like a meeting and more like a high-stakes improv session. Maybe we should all wear name tags so we don't get confused about who's presenting what wild idea next?" A stifled laugh escaped Luna's lips, and even Dr. Evans cracked a smile. The tension eased slightly.

The turning point came during a particularly heated debate about data security. A quiet voice piped up from the back of the room. It was Ms. Hernandez, BioRhythmic's usually reserved receptionist, a self-proclaimed "data security enthusiast" in her free time. Her suggestion for a hybrid encryption protocol that addressed both sides' concerns hung in the air before erupting into a wave of relieved laughter. In that moment, a dam broke. Luna, impressed by Ms. Hernandez's expertise, started looking beyond job titles. HealthNex's engineers, in turn, discovered the value of Luna's meticulous planning, realizing it could expedite the overall workflow.

The once-chaotic brainstorming sessions became a melting pot of ideas. BioRhythmic's Sarah teamed up with HealthNex's graphic designer. The designer, a flamboyant individual with a penchant for neon colors, presented an initial infographic that resembled a rave flyer more than a scientific report. Sarah, raised an eyebrow. "Listen, I love a good dance party as much as the next person, but maybe we tone down the disco ball effect for a more... medically-oriented audience?" The room erupted in laughter, the tension dissolving in a shared moment of amusement. Their combined efforts resulted in a series of infographics that explained the sleep tracker study with both clarity and humor.

Lunch breaks became impromptu strategy sessions, fueled by a mix of BioRhythmic's protein bars and HealthNex's kombucha. During a particularly caffeine-fueled brainstorming session, Sarah glanced around the room at the overflowing coffee cups and cans of sparkling tea. "Anyone else feel like they might need a sleep tracker more than the study participants at this point?" Her comment elicited a round of tired laughter, a reminder of the long hours they were putting in, but also the camaraderie that had blossomed despite their initial challenges. Clara, no longer just a data analyst, became the bridge between the two cultures, valuing everyone's voice and fostering open communication through late-night Slack chats and hallway discussions. Gazing at the team, a kaleidoscope of personalities now working seamlessly, Clara couldn't help but think, "This is what synergy looks like."

CHAPTER 10

Celebrating Milestones

Ms. Thornberry, once CEO of BioRhythmic Devices, now led the merged company. Across from her sat Mr. Peabody, her counterpart from HealthNex Solutions, now serving as Chief Operating Officer. The weight of the past few months hung heavy in the air, but it wasn't the burden of uncertainty; it was the anticipation of success. Their pilot program, a collaboration between BioRhythmic's expertise in data analysis and HealthNex's cutting-edge technology, had exceeded expectations. More importantly, the team, initially a clash of cultures, had begun to function as a cohesive unit.

"We need to capitalize on this momentum, Ms. Thornberry," Mr. Peabody said, his voice betraying a hint of excitement. "These past few months haven't been easy, but the team has come together in a remarkable way."

Ms. Thornberry nodded in agreement. "Absolutely. But how do we ensure this collaboration becomes the norm, not the exception?" she pondered. Their challenge wasn't just about achieving results; it was about building a culture that fostered continuous learning and recognized individual and team achievements.

Their conversation turned to Clara. Her contributions during the pilot program had been invaluable. She had a knack for bridging the gap between HealthNex's established processes and BioRhythmic's innovative spirit. More importantly, she had a genuine respect for her colleagues, fostering open communication and a collaborative environment.

"Clara has the potential to play a key role in reinforcing the desired behaviors and recognizing team members for their achievements," Ms. Thornberry suggested. A thoughtful look settled on Mr. Peabody's face.

"You're right," he conceded. "She has a natural ability to connect with people and inspire them. Perhaps we can create a new initiative that leverages her strengths."

After lunch, Ms. Thornberry invited Clara to her office. Clara entered, a hint of curiosity in her eyes. After a brief exchange about the successful pilot program, Ms. Thornberry got to the point.

"Clara, your contributions to the team have been invaluable. You have a unique ability to bridge divides and create a positive, collaborative environment." Clara blushed slightly, surprised by the praise.

Ms. Thornberry continued, "Mr. Peabody and I believe you could play an even bigger role in the company's future. We're looking to establish a culture that celebrates success and fosters continuous learning. We were wondering if you'd be interested in taking the lead on this initiative?"

Clara's mind raced. Leading a company-wide initiative? It was a daunting proposition, but also an exciting one. The chance to create a more positive and supportive work environment resonated with her.

"I'm… I'm honored," she stammered. "I would love to be involved."

Ms. Thornberry smiled. "Wonderful! We have some initial ideas, but we'd love to hear yours as well. Think about things like recognizing achievements, and encouraging open communication and feedback."

Over the next few days, Clara brainstormed with Ms. Thornberry and Mr. Peabody. Together, they developed a two-pronged approach. First, they established "Milestone Mondays," a company-wide initiative dedicated to highlighting accomplishments, big and small. It could be anything from a successful product launch to a team member exceeding their quota or simply going the extra mile to help a colleague. Recognition, both public and personal, would become a cornerstone of the new company culture.

Second, Clara proposed a program for focused feedback. They encouraged team leaders to schedule one-on-one meetings with their members to discuss performance, not just point out flaws, but also highlight strengths and identify areas for growth. These meetings would offer a platform to assess members' alignment with S.Y.N.E.R.G.Y principles, providing constructive feedback to enhance performance and foster a growth mindset.

Dr. Evans organized a team dinner at a local brewery. It was a relaxed gathering designed to acknowledge the newfound team's efforts and celebrate their joint success.

Ms. Thornberry uncharacteristically, stood on a chair, her glass raised and her voice ringing out above the cheerful chatter. "To the incredible team we've become!" she declared. A roar of "cheers" erupted, the clinking of glasses a symphony of shared victory.

Next to speak was Dr. Evans. With an amused look on his face, he began: "Just a few months ago, when I first entered this room, I was excited about the potential of this team, but I must admit, I didn't fully anticipate the incredible progress we'd make together. Your ability to overcome challenges, embrace new perspectives, and deliver an exceptional project is truly inspiring. Each of you has played a vital role in this success."

Applause erupted, a wave of genuine appreciation washing over the room. Mr. Peabody, his glass held high, echoed Ms. Thornberry's sentiment. "Dr. Evans is right," he boomed, "This team has accomplished something truly remarkable. But the journey doesn't stop here. We need to build on this momentum, learn from both our failures and successes, and celebrate even the smallest victories."

The rest of the evening was a blur of animated conversations, shared stories, and genuine camaraderie. A spirit of unity and shared purpose permeated the room. This wasn't just a team celebrating a successful project; it was a family celebrating the birth of something new, something exciting. A company yet to be named, but a future brimming with possibilities. And at the heart of it all, a quiet data analyst named Clara, no longer so quiet, ready to lead them forward.

CHAPTER 11

Embracing New Horizons

Saturday morning dawned bright and clear, a stark contrast to the storm that had plagued the city for the past few days. Clara, eager to stretch her muscles after a week of work, slipped into her swimsuit and headed for the much-anticipated reopening of the upgraded pool. Pushing through the doors, she was met with a wave of chatter and excitement. Gone were the chipped tiles of the past; the pool shimmered with a fresh, inviting glow. Relief washed over her – finally, a place to unwind.

Unlike her recent ocean explorations, the pool offered a familiar comfort. Clara reveled in the feeling, effortlessly gliding through the water, her worries dissolving with each stroke.

While she had grown surprisingly fond of the unexpected encounters with marine life during her ocean ventures – the flash of silver as a fish darted alongside her, the graceful form of a sea turtle gliding past – there was something undeniably comforting about the predictable serenity of the pool.It was here, in this quiet sanctuary, that Clara allowed her mind to wander.

Her thoughts drifted back to the chaos of the merger. She remembered the initial fear, the uncertainty of her role in the newly formed company. The clash of cultures, the endless meetings, the pressure to prove her worth. But then, there was the unexpected camaraderie, the shared triumphs, and the undeniable sense of accomplishment. She thought of Dr. Evans, the charismatic change management consultant, and his infectious enthusiasm. His metaphors might have been outlandish, but his message had resonated.

Clara smiled. She thought of the S.Y.N.E.R.G.Y. principles and how they had become a guiding star. She'd played a role in shaping the new company culture, fostering collaboration and innovation. The data analyst who once feared becoming obsolete had emerged as a respected voice, a leader. She was no longer just a cog in a machine; she was a vital component, a driving force. The merger hadn't just reshaped the company; it had transformed her. She felt a sense of pride, of accomplishment, that was almost tangible.

Now, floating on her back, watching the world upside down, she felt like a queen of the pool. A queen who'd wrestled a beast and won.

As she climbed out of the pool, a sense of peace washed over her. The physical exertion, combined with the mental clarity, left her feeling refreshed and invigorated. The world outside the pool could wait. For now, there was just her, the warm sun, and the promise of a future filled with endless possibilities.

Emerging from the pool, a fresh towel wrapped around her hair, Clara decided to explore the nearby farmer's market. As she loaded her basket with plump blueberries, tart raspberries, and sun-kissed fragrant strawberries, a familiar voice chuckled beside her. "Looks like you have a thing for berries," it was the man with the fishing rod from her first ocean swim. Her cheeks flushed slightly as she recognized him. "They're for a smoothie," she said, surprised at her own confidence.

He introduced himself as Ben, explaining he enjoyed weekend fishing as a way to unwind and enjoy the fresh catch. His eyes twinkled with amusement as he surveyed the market. "Fresh fish tonight, if you're interested," he offered, pointing to his all too familiar cooler and extending a playful invitation. "I'm a terrible cook, but the fish practically leaps from the water to the pan…well, not really, but it's fresh!"

Clara, feeling a spark of adventure, surprised herself by accepting. Dinner with a charming man who appreciated fresh food? That was definitely not how she envisioned her Saturday night a few months ago. "Fresh fish sounds perfect," she said, her smile widening. "I can bring the berries for dessert."

Back at her building, the elevator doors whooshed open, revealing the former data analyst she'd met a few weeks back. "Clara!" Seamus exclaimed, as she joined him inside. "You look… different. Happy?"

Clara beamed. "There's been a lot of change lately," she admitted, "both at work and personally. It's been… well, exciting!"

He nodded thoughtfully. "Change can be a double-edged sword," he mused. "Uncomfortable at times, but often the catalyst for something wonderful. Embrace it, Clara. It might just lead you to unexpected places." A knowing smile spread across Clara's face as the elevator doors closed. Change already had done just that.

Back in her apartment, the day's events swirled in Clara's mind. Fresh fish, a charming smile, and the promise of a unique evening – what could possibly go wrong? A nervous flutter filled her stomach as she typed out the first line of her text to Michelle: "You won't believe who I met at the market..."

Epilogue: The Roadmap for Navigating Change

Clara stood at the helm of the newly merged company, a powerful entity born from the union of HealthNex's established strength and BioRhythmic Devices' innovative spirit. The journey hadn't been easy, a constant battle against the unpredictable currents of change. But as she surveyed the bustling office, a sense of accomplishment washed over her.

This wasn't just a successful merger; it was a testament to the power of a well-structured approach to change. Looking back, she realized the key principles that had guided them through the storm:

The 7 Cs of Change:

1. Create the Plan: Vision & Goals

The vision, from the very beginning, had been clear: to become a leader in healthcare through the combined expertise of both companies. This vision motivated and united the team. Measurable goals, like joint product development and improved patient outcomes, provided a roadmap for their journey.

2. Communicate about the Plan: Why, What, How

Transparency was paramount. The "why" – the strategic rationale behind the merger – was clearly communicated, emphasizing the benefits for both companies and patients. The "what" – the details of the merger – were outlined with timelines and structure, minimizing surprises and fostering trust. Finally, the "how" – the implementation process – included training plans and open communication channels, ensuring everyone felt heard and involved.

3. Concerns about the Plan

Resistance, like unexpected waves, was inevitable. John's initial skepticism about job security was a case in point. They addressed concerns head-on, facilitating open communication through town halls, Q&A sessions, and anonymous surveys. Additionally, they emphasized the merger's benefits, like career growth opportunities and a more competitive company.

4. Craft Trainings Related to the Plan

They understood that bridging skill gaps was crucial. Training programs were developed to equip employees with the necessary skills, from new technologies to cultural sensitivity. Collaboration workshops encouraged teamwork, breaking down cultural barriers and fostering a sense of unity.

5. Culture that Supports the Plan

Building a culture that embraced their values was a continuous effort. They identified behaviors that aligned with those values which, together, created synergy between the two companies.

6. Call to Action/Implementation

Employee engagement was the engine that propelled them forward. Task forces were formed to solicit ideas and knowledge-sharing, keeping everyone actively involved.

7. Celebrate Milestones: Reinforcements: Feedback, Rewards, Recognition

Celebrating wins, big and small, kept everyone motivated. Milestones, such as system integration and team collaboration successes, were recognized, reinforcing positive behaviors. Feedback and reward systems were implemented, acknowledging contributions and fostering a sense of accomplishment.

The 7 Cs served as their compass, guiding them through uncharted waters. The merger wasn't just about efficiency; it was about transformation. As Clara looked out the window, the city lights twinkling like a promise, she knew this was just the beginning. Change, like the ocean, would be a constant companion. But now, they had the tools, the team, and the unwavering spirit to navigate any current that came their way. Their journey, a testament to the power of strategic change, had just begun.

Applying the 7 Cs of Change: A Guide for Navigating Your Own Transformation

Clara and her team successfully navigated the turbulent waters of change by embracing the 7 Cs. You can too. Here's how:

Create the Plan: Vision & Goals

- **Define your vision:** What do you want to achieve? Is it increased efficiency, improved employee morale, or a new product launch?

- **Set clear goals:** Break down your vision into actionable steps. Make them specific, measurable, achievable, relevant, and time-bound (SMART).

Communicate about the Plan: Why, What, How

- **Transparency is key:** Clearly articulate the "why" behind the change. Employees are more likely to support a change they understand.

- **Provide clear details:** Outline the "what" and "how" of the change process. Transparency builds trust and reduces anxiety.

Address Concerns and Resistance

- **Open communication channels:** Create forums for employees to voice concerns and suggestions.

- **Emphasize benefits:** Highlight how the change will positively impact employees and the organization.

- **Address resistance directly:** Acknowledge concerns and provide solutions or explanations.

Craft Relevant Trainings

- **Identify skill gaps:** Assess your team's needs to determine necessary training.

- **Develop targeted training programs:** Offer training that directly supports the change initiative.

- **Foster collaboration:** Encourage knowledge sharing and teamwork through training.

Build a Supportive Culture

- **Define shared values:** Identify core values that align with the change initiative.

- **Celebrate achievements:** Recognize and reward employees for their contributions.

- **Foster a positive work environment:** Create a culture of trust, respect, and inclusivity.

Engage Your Team

- **Involve employees:** Seek input and ideas from all levels of the organization.

- **Form task forces:** Create cross-functional teams to drive the change initiative.

- **Empower employees:** Give employees ownership and responsibility for the change process.

Celebrate Milestones and Seek Feedback

- **Recognize achievements:** Acknowledge and celebrate milestones along the way.

- **Gather feedback:** Use surveys, one-on-one meetings, or focus groups to assess progress and identify areas for improvement.

- **Reward and recognize contributions:** Show appreciation for employees' efforts and dedication.

Remember: Change is a journey, not a destination. Embrace the process, learn from challenges, and celebrate successes. By applying the 7 Cs of Change, you can navigate your organization's transformation with confidence and resilience.

Reflection Questions:

- How can I apply these principles to my specific change initiative?

- What are the potential challenges I might face, and how can I address them?

- How can I measure the success of my change initiative?

By reflecting on these questions and consistently applying the 7 Cs, you can lead your organization through successful change.

Navigate Change with Confidence

Inspired by the transformative journey in *Currents of Change?*

Dr. Sharon Grossman, the guiding hand behind this fable, offers tailored solutions to help your organization thrive amidst change.

From team building retreats to executive coaching and trainings, Dr. Grossman provides expert guidance to unlock your team's full potential.

Ready to navigate the currents? Contact Dr. Sharon Grossman at www.drsharongrossman.com

Also by Sharon Grossman

The Solution to Burnout: 7 Steps from Exhausted to Extraordinary

How to Train Your Brain for Success in 5 Steps

The Stress Advantage: Lessons from the Tennis Court

Wheely Good Team Building: A Rollerskating Retreat to Revive a Company

About the Author

Dr. Sharon Grossman is a powerhouse of productivity. With over 20 years of experience as a therapist and executive coach, she leverages her psychology background to empower individuals and teams. Dr. Grossman is not only the author of several books, but also a sought-after business consultant and keynote speaker.

Through her company, The Productivity Trainers, Dr. Grossman's mission is clear: to guide teams from overwhelmed to optimal performance, all without burning out.

When she's not helping teams reach their full potential, Sharon enjoys life in Miami Beach, Florida with her husband and two children.

Connect with Dr. Sharon:

- Website: www.DrSharonGrossman.com
- LinkedIn: @sharongrossman